Sometimes Women Lie About Being Okay

Sometimes Women Lie About Being Okay

Poems and Sketches

By

Rachel Joy Welcher

Copyright © 2022 by Rachel Joy Welcher
Dustlings Press, Vermillion, South Dakota

For Winnie

Poetry is my love language,
my lament language,
my way of wrapping hope
around a fig tree.

Table of Contents

Rain in the Midwest

Rain in the Midwest..17-18
My Pack..19
Adult Life..20
Ash Wednesday...21
Notes From My Old Survival Guide..22
Calm and Corduroy...23
A Reminder..24
Yellow Irises...25
Ode to the Weighted Blanket...26
I Forgive You...27
A Prayer for the Weary..28
Terra...29
Jack..30
Do Not Wait...31
Sunset..32
Selah...33
The New House...34
A Kind of Hope..35

The Happiness Machine

The Happiness Machine...39-40
Ice Cream or Tragedy..41
Angels..42

Bonfire Friends..43
A Circle...44
1 Kings 19...45
Listen..46
Not Pregnant (Again)..47
King..48
Grocery List Heretic...49
Windows Down..50
This...51
Silly Love Poem..52
Before Even Getting to See Your Face.............53
Never Hiding..54
My First Mother's Day......................................55
One Second...56
Competition for the Maples.............................57
Longsuffering...58-59

By the Rivers of Babylon

By the Rivers of Babylon..............................63-64
The Cave...65-66
English Ivy..67
In the cool of the day....................................68-69
Winnie Mae...70
Three..71-72
Green...73
Maternity Shorts...74-75
Sad, Together...76-78
A Kindness..79

The Tree of Knowledge...80
Good Things That Are Still Good Even When Your
Heart is Breaking..81-82
If You Ask Me About Today...83
Hope..84
When Grief Soaks the Ground.......................................85

Praying for Birds

Grain Offerings...89-90
The Mother..91
My Child..92
String of Lights...93-94
Hildegaard...95
Trees, Caves, and Houses...96
All My Dreams..97
Murder..98
New Faith Rising...99-100
Eleven Percent...101
Vows..102-103
Praying for Birds..104-106
Vapors...107-108
The Plague..109
A Prayer for Those Waiting for the Other Shoe to
Drop..110-111
Everest..112
Being Known..113-114
Know This..115
Planter Box...116-117

You..118
The Finale of Grief.................................119-120

Acknowledgements..123

About the Author..125

Rain in the Midwest

Rain in the Midwest

On rare days when it rained in Southern California, my grandpa would take his pillow out to the trailer in the backyard and sleep there, just to hear the raindrops hitting the tin roof.

It made him happy, and I've always liked this about him, the way he wanted to hear the rain. I can't say I understood it until I moved to the Midwest, where rain is more like a vertical river than a California shower.

It comes down in sheets and waves and the sound fills your bedroom at night. And in the early morning. And in the middle of the day, the thunder booms and the air is wet but warm.

My grandpa grew up in Indiana and took bike trips with his brothers in the summer, carrying only potatoes and postcards in their pockets. Each time they reached a new town, they would put a postcard in the mail to their mother and find someone's barn to sleep in. In the morning, the family who owned the barn would invite them in for breakfast.

"Those were the days," he would say. And these are the stories I miss now that he's gone. Sometimes it starts to rain when I'm painting outside. I listen to the sound it makes when it hits the overhang on our porch and I watch it flood my garden, and I think, these are the sights and sounds he grew up with. I watch and listen as I use the paint brushes he gave me, the ones he broke in over years and years of creating beautiful scenes and trying to show me how to add texture to trees and streams, and how to give a rock its shadow. I miss him. I listen to the rain, and I miss him. I paint, and I miss him.

But I'm getting better at painting clouds. And I think he would like the way I add light to tree branches. He would say, "That's real good, sweetie," and we'd paint together in the trailer in the backyard, where he kept half his art supplies. And he would show me which brush was best for whatever I wanted to paint next.

My Pack

You bring the dog with you
when you think I'm sad.
I hear the stairs creak and
Frank's collar jingle
as you travel, as a pack,
to our upstairs bedroom
where I lie reading my phone
on our bed, in the dark.

I say: "Hey baby. And Frank!"
And you say, "Are you sad?"
And I say, "I told you I wasn't."
And you reply, "Yes, but sometimes
women lie about being okay."
And that's true.

Sometimes we do.

Adult Life

The entire adult life is
one long attempt to shame
your high school crush
for not loving you back.

Ash Wednesday

All it takes
is one pine tree with heavy cones,
slouching and rain-worn in the California fog
to commiserate and give me that calm
before the storm. I grip my toes like roots
digging into the soil of this thing that you are asking
of me. I pray, obeying my yoga teacher as I stack
my vertebrae like imaginary blocks, righting
myself from the twisted position I have been
sleeping in, asking you:

"Will you let me shake and flourish
at the same time? Will you water
me without drowning me? Please.
Do not go far. I am dust.
Remember?
I am dust.

Notes From My Old Survival Guide

I'm sorry.
You're right.
I'm sorry.
Yes. You're right.
I get it. You're right.
You're right.
You're right.
You're right.
I'm sorry. You're right.
I'm sorry.
Right.
Of course.
Yes.
You're right.
No, it was me. It's my fault.
I misunderstood.
I remembered it wrong.
You're right.
Yes, I understand. You're right.
You're right.
You're right.
I'm sorry.
I'm sorry.
I'm sorry.
I'm sorry.
I'm sorry.

Calm and Corduroy

So much of what I thought
my life would be was
burned up in a flash.

The smoke choked
my expectations
for the future.

But then, you.

You, in all your calm,
and humor and corduroy charm.

You, in your brave kindness,
and *Pearl Jam* lyrics.

You, encircling me with your arms
of crackling fireplace warmth
in the dead of winter,

showing me that the
unexpected is often better
than the things we plan out
in ink, on paper.

A Reminder

I saw a nest in the tree
between my neighbor's house
and mine while I was rinsing out
the coffee pot this morning;

a reminder that life keeps living,
growing, and building homes
in the branches of trees,
without my effort.

Maybe we need to sleep-in
more often, absorb the
kindness of the sun
on our faces.
A reminder that it will rise
and warm us, whether
we notice it or not.

We do not have to will
the day to start.
It begins without us,
and there is some relief in that,
I think. Some small exhale and
shifting of the invisible weight
we all carry, as we try to balance
the world on our shoulders.

Yellow Irises

When the rains come in the Midwest
early spring flowers take a beating.
Their heads bow down low
to the ground, and their petals
lose their weightlessness.

Is this the punishment
eagerness deserves?

My yellow irises try to lift
their heavy heads, and shake off
the lingering droplets. I can only
hope that their roots were fed,
instead of drowned.

Why does the sun make promises
the rain can't keep?

Foolish flowers, all of them,
thinking it was safe
to unfold their petals
and open up.

Ode to the Weighted Blanket

It presses down on my rising
panic, weight conquering weight
like twin brothers, sumo wrestling.
How can heaviness do the heavy
lifting, or make the weight of life
which tries to drown me, float? I
take a breath as I reach the surface,
fighting the anchor tied to my ankle.
It is the even distribution of weight? The
free will choice of the matter? These
are questions I ask but never answer
because, by the time I pull the blanket
over my body, my aching bones and
anxious questions quiet down, and
I am already half-asleep.

I Forgive You ✷

is a poem when
the words have
taken this long
to write.

A Prayer for the Weary

May God prepare a table for us
in the wilderness of our future,
manna, in the deserts of our past,
and wine from vineyards that we
burned down in anger, frustration
and disappointment, in our longing
for what once was, and what we hoped
would be. Father, spread a feast
right here, where we stand, legs weak
from fleeing temptation, arms tired
from holding one another's grief,
voices hoarse from crying out
for justice and your return.
Quench our thirst,
read our minds,
heal our wounds,
thaw our hearts,
with a Love that never leaves.

Terra

I stole a tree
from my parent's yard
this winter; a newborn
California blue spruce with
roots the color of turnips.

My husband helped me
dig it up, and before we
sealed it in a zip-lock bag, and
shoved it into our suitcase, I
sprinkled some red clay dirt
inside, the kind I turned into
pies and pots and bug homes
as a kid, hoping that when it
is replanted in my backyard in Iowa
it will feel a little more
like home.

Jack
For a friend

It snowed in April
the morning you were born,
not heavy or slippery,
but soft, like eyelashes,
covering our budding town
in weightless white.

The world shifted
like a mother with a baby
on her hip, switching her weight
from foot to foot, rocking
out a rhythm, a song, for you.

We all changed that morning,
a blanket of snow on our homes,
a song humming from your
mother's lips, and you,
here with us, real and true,
squirming with life.

Do Not Wait

Do not wait to rejoice.
Do not wait to enjoy.
Do not save and save
and forget to spend yourself
walking up a tall hill just for
the view. Do not say:
"When it is quiet, I will..."
Find the quiet. Chase it.
Walk to where the quiet lives,
and pray while watching a bird
hop on the ground. Do not worry
about bringing a pen
or taking a picture.
It is meant to be fleeting,
a vapor, a brief moment
to reintroduce yourself to God.

Sunset is the thing with motives
as pure as gold, spinning glitter
while asking me to trust her

to sit and watch my hands
turn yellow, then pink,
then dark, dark purple, while I
sip the air like wine - why

does the cold always hit
my face out of nowhere? How
did the sun slip away
without my notice?

I look up, and the trees
have become silhouettes,
cold, frayed wires, and I
remember, with a shake
and shiver, the last time
that I tried to find my way home
in the dark.

Selah

Is there anything more pure
than a young girl catching
tadpoles in the rainwater
caught in an old canoe?
This one has legs!
She yells, scooping water
into her hands, like a home.

The New House

They worked on that house for months and
visited the wilderness of their property
every night for years, dreaming about
what could be built up among the red dirt
and manzanita trees. Even still, their first
night in the house, the beautiful house,
my mom texted me: "Everyone talks about
how great high ceilings are, but they aren't cozy."
The next night: "Elliot is hiding under
your dad's recliner." A week in, I asked
"Does it feel like home yet?" and she replied:
"It's wonderful, but I'm still getting used to it."
And that is how all new things begin, lonely
at first, even in the joy of newness, alongside
the smell of fresh paint, there is the occasional
alien shiver, as if it was the clutter and dust that
was softening the echoes the entire time.
New is good. New is necessary.
It just takes
some getting used to.

But we'll get there.

A Kind of Hope

Got up at 3 a.m. and from
my bathroom window saw
the first firefly of the season,
blinking, mid-air and alone,
in the middle of a rainstorm.

The Happiness Machine

The Happiness Machine

It wasn't until Leo Auffman was almost done building his Happiness Machine that I noticed Evan had his good ear down on the pillow.

I've been reading him chapters from Ray Bradbury's *Dandelion Wine* at night. Tonight, he is smiling at me through sleepy eyes, rolled up in our winter blanket like a burrito. I thought his smile was due to the magic of Bradbury's descriptions – especially of summertime in the Midwest – but it turns out he has just been watching my lips, happy and half-deaf, content to be read to by his wife, whose voice couldn't sound like more than a muffled hum.

Now his eyes are all the way closed.

"Babe, are you listening?"

"I can hear. Leo Aufferman is doing something."

"Leo *Auffman*."

"Yeah. He's building a thing."

"A Happiness Machine, babe. He's building a Happiness Machine. Only it's making his whole family miserable, when they were perfectly happy before. Isn't that ironic?"

He doesn't respond, but continues to smile with his eyes closed, listening to the hum of my voice. It isn't about the story for him.

Maybe the only reason he says yes when I ask him: "Do you want me to read you a chapter tonight?" is because he sees how much I love this book. And maybe he thinks I miss reading aloud to my high school students. Maybe I do. Or maybe I miss an experience I've never had – reading to my own children. He knows it makes me happy to think I'm re-creating the experience my aunt gave me and my siblings when she read this book to us, crowded around her on the bed, one summer, years ago.

He knows me better than I think. I look at him, and he's still smiling.

How can I resist? I grab his hands in both of mine and kiss his forehead, his cheek, and his arm. Then I sigh in fake exasperation, dog-ear the page, take off my glasses, and turn out the light.

Ice Cream or Tragedy

Faithfulness is the sound of
my husband shovelling the snow
off our front steps before putting
on his tie and jacket for church.

It is the hum of the coffee maker
at 6:30 a.m., before my feet
have even touched the bedroom floor.

It is this: that when we sigh and push
one another's buttons, as they say,
I know he'll stay, and tomorrow morning
when I am still half asleep, he will pray
over us, for our day, and our life together.

And though so many things are fragile,
we will not break, because the steadiness
beneath our feet is God, the Creator,
the Author; the opposite of shifting sand,
we stand with hands interlaced, tightly,
ready for ice cream or tragedy,
whichever comes first.

Angels

There is nothing better
than eating cinnamon rolls
with you at 10 p.m.

things into which
angels long to look.

Bonfire Friends

Sometimes I wish that we
had been young together;
lizard-chasing, ball-catching,
pool-splashing, costume-wearing
young. Or maybe, that we had met
at summer camp and been tan
and laughing, sunscreen-sharing,
Bible-skit-acting, bonfire friends.
Or that we had gone to the prom
together as high school sweethearts,
or at least that we were each other's
college crush. First marriage? It's okay,
we say, because those years and
people mattered. So much. And
those experiences made us who
we are today, for the world and
for each other. But it is also okay,
I think, to dream about what it
would have been like to
have known you forever.
That foreign ache I felt
throughout my teens and twenties
of grief catching in my throat,
it makes sense now.

I was missing you for decades.

A Circle

I walked the perimeter
of the pond this afternoon,
disturbing the frogs until they leapt
like dominos into the water,
one so big it barked like a dog –
I imagine – to alert the others.

But all I did was give them
the chance, by shock and
water, to remember
that we are alive.

1 Kings 19

You are the God of cake
baked on hot stones, resting
above Elijah's head, the One
who knows our frame, that we
are made of dust. You give us
milk and honey, and grapes
bursting on our tongues, wine
rich, red, earthy, heart-gladdening
wine. Our cups tremble under
the weight of this mercy.

For the journey is too great
without this sustenance, without
the bread and the wine, your
body and your blood, broken,
buried, and raised, you feed us
stomach and soul, in the very
moment we had resigned ourselves
to give up.

Listen

Listen to the low hum of our house
at midnight. Listen to the curtains
drawn, the dishwasher finishing
up its 11 p.m. load like a champ.
Listen to the sound of our collective
peace, as old, creaky steps settle, and we
finally give in to sleep after a day
of questions with no answers.

When we wake up, we will stretch
our arms and take a moment to
watch the steam coming off our
second cup of coffee. We will pause
before the day gets going, and we
lose ourselves in its details. We
will acknowledge, for a brief moment,
how exhausting this life is,
but beautiful.

Not Pregnant (Again) ✶

I would like a good reason for this tiredness,
this plump belly that makes me self-conscious in all my
dresses, the Rory to my Loreleigh - I won't ever know what
that is like.
To wish my daughter could come home for Christmas. To
read her all my favorite children's books and teach her how
to paint. This pain grows more severe every month, I should
probably see a doctor about that, but I keep hoping that at
some point it will become life-giving pain, that
this part of my life and body have been building up to
something worthwhile. Instead, I see one line again.
One line.
Never two.
And that's fine, if only it didn't mean
that I'll never get to meet you.

King

First night in the king bed,
and you are oceans away.
If I turn, will the movement
ripple out to you, a message
in a bottle, telling you that I
am okay? I made it to the edge
of the mattress and back and
found that I love swimming
myself to sleep, knowing
that you are always
within reach.

Grocery List Heretic

What would an honest poem
about marriage look like?
It would include your socks,
of course, scattered on the floor,
fuelling stereotypes and memes
about men and marriage, but it
would also include the grocery lists
I text you, that you follow religiously,
and add to, heretically,
surprising me with my favorite things,
like yellow flowers and fancy cheese,
dark chocolate, and most recently,
a Christmas tree. You never make me
feel like a burden that is too heavy to lift.

Windows Down

I want to give you the breeze
moving through an oak tree
for every day you have suffered,
a perfectly ripe mango for
every day you have grieved,
the peace that comes from
evenings and tidepools and
driving past corn fields with
the windows down in your truck,
for every day that you have
experienced the weight
of this world.
Every day with you is
a privilege. Every moment,
an honor.

This

I ran through the rain
to tell you our invisible
secret. You grabbed my
hand and led me to
the front of the church

where we kneeled in
smiling disbelief,
my heart beating
so fast, your lips
praying, "Thank you,
God, for this."

Silly Love Poem

I want to build
a pillow fort
in the comfort of
your presence.

I want to write
"Rachel Welcher"
on all my middle school
notebooks, with scribbled
hearts and love notes.

I want you
all the days
of my life.

Before Even Getting to See Your Face

Today, I think I might lose you.

I'm bleeding a little. They say
it's nothing to worry about.
They say it's normal. But I
can't help but see you
slipping through my fingers
before even getting the chance
to kiss your face, smell your head,
and name you. Does it ever feel
like Happiness is just holding
her breath? That Joy, when she
comes in the morning, pours
the coffee with shaking hands?

I wonder if it ever gets easier
to hope.

Never Hiding

You find something to love
about every place and thing,
saying, "I could live here,"
"We should build
something like that,"
or, "I would wear that hat,"
and I marvel
at the way you approach life,
never hiding
from the pain,
never hiding
from the joy.

My First Mother's Day

A phone app tells me
you're the size of a
sesame seed and that
your heart will soon
begin beating. I feel a
twinge in my belly
and don't know if I
should cry with joy or
hold my breath.

All I know is that
last night I woke
up at 2 a.m.
smiling.

One Second

On ordinary days, when the
part you bought to fix the toilet
doesn't work, and I'm editing poems
with a headache, and we pass one
another in the living room,
and you slap me on the rump and
say, "I'm going to have to go back
to the hardware store tomorrow,"
and we sigh and joke that we are
already too old in our thirties,
with aching backs, an affinity for naps.
and staying home

and I wouldn't trade one second
of one ordinary day with you
for one hundred extraordinary days
somewhere else,

that's the truth.

And that's the poem.

Competition for the Maples

The yellow irises
unfurled today
in honor of you.

They stand bright
among the sucker trees
and budding maples,
short-lived in their glory.

A moment of spring
in the panic of this pandemic.

And one day I will
show them to you,
as I will show you
the entire garden, if
only you would
keep growing,
beloved one.

Give the maples
some competition
because I can't wait
to meet you.

Longsuffering

I kick at the sheets of this day
while you sleep. And I think
back to a time before I said "yes"
to you, when I was asking
questions like a hurricane.

I asked your closest friends:
*What one word would you use
to describe him?*

Longsuffering,
they said.

Two words, forced together
by your example. And I realize
that I have never met anyone
who suffers so long the
windstorms of life, the questions,
the funerals, and the complaints that
skip like a broken record. Instead of
giving up, you throw another log
onto the fire and let it burn until
the moon comes out.

When you sigh, you shift the weight
for all of us, creating room for peace.

And in the morning,

you meet His new mercies
on a gravel path where the sunlight
is just beginning to warm the rocks.

You pray for the world, then pull
your hands inside your coat
and walk back home to drink three
cups of coffee, just to greet me,
sleepy and smiling.

By the Rivers of Babylon

By the Rivers of Babylon

An imaginative reading of Psalm 137

By the rivers of Babylon we sit and weep. I scoop water into my hands and splash it over my face. Shock and ice. Relief and purity. My hands need this coolness, this shiver, for they throb under constant use. I run my fingers across the calluses that have formed. My hands ache the way my heart aches. An instrument I used to love to play now feels like a slavedriver. I strum the songs of my youth, but lately, I play them through tears.

There on the poplars we hang our harps. An act of silent protest. We will not play for you today. I look and see my sister sitting among the reeds, knees hugged to chest, rocking back and forth. She is in pain, remembering Zion. We long for freedom. The days when we were not forced to sing and dance for the very ones who killed our father. We watched him die, both of us. I will never forget the look on his face. He couldn't breathe, but no one cared. I have written songs about this, *but our tormentors demand songs of joy.*

So we sneak away to the water's edge. We talk in whispers, laughing and crying softly. One of us begins a low hum, a song of lament. Others join, and together, our voices form a single prayer: *O Lord, how long? Do not forget your people.* Our songs belong to us alone. *Do not leave us in exile. Do not forsake justice.* We will not share them. The songs we sing when we are alone, together, cannot be sold, analyzed, or parsed for meaning, only sung in wailing harmony. Melodies of protest, lyrics of freedom.

    I know that tomorrow, I must pick up my harp again and perform for my captors. I sigh, steadying myself, patting down my hair, and massaging my hands. I wonder, *how can we sing the songs of the Lord while in a foreign land?* But they do not own my voice. I will change the words, sing in the same happy melody that keeps them pacified and charms them with my culture, but I will sing to God alone: *Your kingdom come. Your sword be sharp. Your will be done. Your justice swift. Bring heaven down to earth, and soon. If I forget you, Jerusalem...*I will not forget you. They will not win.

The Cave

There is a small cave
in the side of a mountain
near Priest Lake, Idaho
that has been hollowed out
by a waterfall that swells
each year when the snow
melts.

The river rushes
and crashes into her,
shaping her body
into an empty tomb.

Only time
and repetition could give
something as soft as water
the power
to wear down something
as strong as stone.

We visit this scene
in the daytime,
laughing and taking pictures
of pine trees and eddies,
splashing one another, asking
*"How many bats do you think
live in there?"* pointing to the

hollow darkness of her belly
as if it could ever be a home.

English Ivy

I have discovered that
English ivy can grow
with very little water
as long as there is Light.

In the Cool of the Day

All I've ever wanted is to walk
with You in the cool of the day
like Adam and Eve did before
the fall of our hearts, to feel moss
under my feet, and Your voice,
holy, holy, wholly present.
Before sweet fruit turned bitter,
and our eyes beheld things
our arms could never lift. You
knew what goodness meant for us
and we doubted that. I still do
sometimes. I'm sorry.

All I've ever wanted is to talk
with You under the sun, to
tell You how much I love the
things you have made, how
the maple tree buds at the exact
moment I needed spring,
and the porch cat jumps
onto my lap to soften the
sharpness of grief.

You knew. You know. You are
the God of maple trees and
broken hearts. Of lilies and
sparrows, sand, and hair. You

hold our joy and lament with
equal care. All I've ever wanted
is to thank You for that, to stand
in that ancient garden and pray.

Winnie Mae

I wanted to meet you and
see the shape of your mouth.
I wanted to smell your head,
and name you Winnie Mae.
I know we must live with hands
open to God, but I really thought
He would let me hear your heart
beat today.

Three

Yesterday was a long night.

My facemask fell down to my chin
when I tried untangling the IV cord
from my hospital gown. The nurse

said, "you need to pull that back up,"
as if I were an anti-masker
instead of an almost-mother, and I
felt embarrassed
and fragile.

When the ER doctor came in,
she asked "How many is this?"
and I told her, "Three."

"Three children?" she asked.
"Yes," I said. But still,
she kept looking at me.

"Any *living* children?"
she asked. It must have been
a box she needed to check.

"Oh," I said,
adjusting my mask,
"No," I said,
understanding what

she had asked.

And I listened to the sound
her pen made as she
scratched out my answer.

Green

I knew summer all winter long,
green in my window,
protected by frosty glass.
This is how the spirit lives,
how it survives an Iowa winter,
the sticks and snow, and the
humble routine of putting on boots
and gloves just to walk
to the mailbox. My spearmint plant
grows in a wild tangle, as though
the sun is always warm,
even from this great distance.

Maternity Shorts

arrived in the mail today,
two weeks late.

I'll never understand
life dangled like
hope-bait, birthing in us
new dreams, only to
lead to a dead end.

We weep.

But the shorts still fit
my swollen stomach,
soft and stretched,
ready to carry you.

Two weeks ago,

I was planning
your nursery.

He was researching
mini vans.

Two weeks ago
we were settling into
the idea of you,

your tiny heart,

and budding limbs.

And all the things
we wanted to show you.

Sad, Together

For two months, every time I woke up in the middle of the night, I made sure to drink water. I had read somewhere how important it is to avoid dehydration in the first trimester. Apparently, your blood volume increases significantly when you are pregnant. I kept picturing that water conservation sketch from Sesame Street - the one where the fish in the pond is losing water, and he calls the boy who is inside the house to ask him to turn off the faucet while he's brushing his teeth - remember that one? In my imagination, our baby was like a tiny fish, and I wanted to give her all the life-giving fluid she needed.

While we were both up, I talked to her, knowing her ears had yet to be fully formed. Knowing I might never get to meet her. Knowing that she was this tiny miracle of a soul whose future I had no control over. It was strange, beautiful, and short-lived. But in that span of time, everything I did revolved around her. What I ate. When I ate. How long I spent in the garden with the sun beating down on my back. I readily gave in to naps, assuming she was asking me to slow down, and that I should listen.

We don't talk about miscarriage much. It's a strange grief - too small to bury in a coffin - but strong enough to break your heart. We planted sunflowers. They are already growing, but she is not. I would be "showing" by now, finally able to wear that dress I bought that hugs my belly. I still find myself caressing my stomach, in moments of forgetfulness.

It's been a few weeks since we lost her. I find those midnight trips to the bathroom so empty now. For a short while, even having to get up to pee at night seemed to have a higher purpose. Isn't that strange? I was a vessel, and she was the boss. I walked through Target to grab some dog food the other day. I passed through the craft section, the one with crisp journals and poster boards and pretty tape. It broke me. A reminder of all the things I was so excited to show her. An imagined future, now fiction.

Love is always a risk. I think about trying again. About the disappointment of negative pregnancy tests. Evan's face when I ran through the rain to the church to tell him we were pregnant. That drop in the pit of my stomach when I realized I was bleeding. The mountains and slopes of hope.

Then I think about when Evan and I first started talking. I was still in so much pain from my divorce. He was still healing from the loss of his wife. "We should take this very slow," I kept telling myself, and him. "Whatever you need. I'm not going anywhere," he would tell me. And I believe he would have waited years for me.

But my plan of waiting, of exhausting every single question, and doing everything I could to avoid the risk of future pain dissolved in a matter of months. He was it. That was clear. And we didn't want to wait to be happy. And in a way, we didn't want to wait to be sad either, if it meant being sad, together.

A Kindness

Our garden gave us
orange day lilies early
this year. I saw them

peeking through the
sucker trees from my
spot among the ashes.

We are never forgotten.

The Tree of Knowledge

Few know that
the Weeping Willow
used to go by another name.

She had hopeful branches then,
with leaves that grew toward the sun.

Her spine glittered with sap
and curiosity, the content kind,
that doesn't need to be satisfied.

Her fruit was ripe and untouched,
appearing to contain every color at once.

On hot summer days, when her branches
weep, she remembers, in flashes,
what it was like

before her name changed,
before her second christening,

before her arms became so heavy
from the weight of living,
that they let down all
her fruit at once.

Good Things That Are Still Good Even When Your Heart Is Breaking

The rabbit who lives in my yard
and comes out to eat his evening
meal of clovers at dusk.

The feel of a fresh notebook

Coffee.

Ben & Jerry's ice cream.
Any flavor,
but mostly *Half-Baked*.

The lighting bugs who
wait in the grass during the
day and come out at night
to wink their love.

Baby toes.

Baby giggles.

Baby wonder.

A brand-new sweater
at the beginning of fall,
the kind you can lose
your hands inside.

Kraft macaroni and cheese.

A text from my best friend.

A text from my mom.

A text from anyone who is
not actively breaking my heart.

New paints.

If You Ask Me About Today

I will ask you if you remember
that ride at the county fair, the one
that smelled like popcorn and vomit;
a room spinning so hard and with so
many mirrors that it felt like the floor
was dropping out
beneath your feet.

Even after the ride stopped and you
wobbled back out into the sunshine
to breathe in fresh air and the scent
of funnel cake and sunscreen, there
was a continued sense of movement,
a dizzy fear that, at any moment, you
might lose your balance, and
be swallowed whole by the ground
opening wide and deep
beneath your feet.

Hope

The birds know it's spring
before I do.

They dance in the grey mist
and chatter about

some fresh, blackberry future
that I cannot see.

When Grief Soaks the Ground

It wasn't until I saw
the land you had tilled,
the dirt lining the sidewalk
leading to our house, that I
cried. Really cried. Realizing
that she will be sunflowers,
but never in my arms. Lord,
this feels like too much.

We plant seeds and pray, telling You
we trust You. And we do. We always
have, but this hurts. And we tell You
that, too. I am still bleeding from her
death as we push dirt into mounds,
telling one another for the hundredth
time this week: I love you. I love you, too.
And our grief soaks the ground, so
that we do not drown.

We will never forget you.

Praying for Birds

Grain Offerings

An imaginative reading of Leviticus chapter 2.

I imagine the griddle heating up in the receding dark. It is early morning and a young mother yawns, searching her kitchen for the flour she set aside. The flour that has been sifted over and over again - fine - like dust. She has hidden it on the highest shelf. The one her children can't reach.

She sifts the flour again, one more time, letting it fall like a heap of snow on the counter, powdering her dress. She marvels at the worship of this task, in the quiet morning of her kitchen. She arose early, just for this. To capture the stillness that the sunrise steals away. To let herself bake this cake slowly. The bread that will be offered to God.

She smiles through tears. It has been a weary week, but God has continued His mercy. Her tiredness and joy mingle together as she pours out the oil like a prayer. Aaron may be the one to crumble this grain offering before God, but she is the one who smooths the dough, stretching it tight to create the perfect crust.

Add salt to all your offerings, she reminds herself, dusting the cake with flavor. This bread is for God.

Her littlest one smells the cakes and hears the oil crackling. She stretches her tiny limbs, rises from her cot, and wanders over to her mother, hugging her legs. She wonders what is for breakfast.

Add salt to all your offerings because Aaron and his sons will eat a portion. This is how we honor God. This is how we care for His people. With warm cakes made from the finest flour. She bends down and smooths her daughter's hair.

Add salt to all your offerings. Knead the dough of worship. Sprinkle the flavor of praise.

The night before Easter, I trimmed the stems off eighty flowers, arranging them in a bowl. The next morning, children, with grandparents, fathers, and sons all grabbed a stem and walked them up to the cross, where they placed them strategically, to fill in all the gaps, until the entire cross was flowered. Until the only wood we could see was the base, covered in yellow, peeling paint. Until the flowers took on the shape of Calvary. An offering, in the early morning, to God.

The Mother

The feral cat is nesting, sneaking
into small spaces, dark places, searching
for somewhere to have her young. She
refuses the house we built her, with
the hole cut to size, the hay, which the
internet told us would keep her warm.
Instead, she runs past our ankles when
we open the door and races upstairs
to our bedroom closet. She has chosen.
She knows what she wants. We try to
change her mind, but there is no force
quite as stubborn and holy as a mother.

My Child

Even a faint blue line
means you're mine,
on earth as it is
in heaven.

String of Lights

Me:
You know those lights
we string between trees
and wooden posts and
outside at evening weddings?
The ones that make
ordinary days and places
twinkle with magic, cutting
through the dim with
unexpected celebration?

You are my string of lights.

You bring joy and light
to the back porch of life.

Him:
You know those lights
Shining in the midst of
Rolling blackouts
Here & There
Cutting through the Din
And the dingy
Of life down here
Shining like the Lord's
Stars
How... they're outside

But have to be plugged in
And how,
This Love Has Been Shocking
Because Goodness Remains.

Hildegaard

The medicine that is keeping you
inside me is keeping me awake. Up
at 3 am, sitting on the couch with
both cats on my lap. We don't
turn the television on. We don't tweet.
Instead, we listen to the wind and snow
outside, our first South Dakota winter,
and you could arrive at any time.
You'll be early, but you'll be mine.

Trees, Caves, and Houses

You left a tree on my belly,
branches stretching upward
toward my heart; creating a map
to the forest of my voice
where we will meet with
Edmund and Lucy,
Anne and Gilbert,
Tigger and Roo,

and I will stare at you
until you fall asleep
and for a long while after that,
my Dearest Girl, the one
who turned my body
from a cave
into a home.

All My Dreams

All my dreams now are about
losing you, trying to find
where I put you down to sleep
then following your cries like a
game of "hot" and "cold."

I wake up wrestling with the sheets,
as though you were lost in the ocean of them.

I wake up jolting toward your bassinet
scanning for your small frame in the dark,
swaddled like an inchworm.

I bend down and scoop you up, press
my face into your warmth like I would
a bath towel straight from the dryer, then
unravel you from your cocoon.

You put your baby arms around my neck
and rest your head on my shoulder,
still half-asleep, hands scrunching
the fabric around my collar.

You hold on for dear life,
breathing in the smell of my *Dove* soap
and *L'Oréal* shampoo. I don't know
what you dreamed about, but
as you hold onto me, I hold onto you.

Murder

Before having a child,
I considered myself a pacifist.

But the violence I feel
toward the mosquito who
just bit my daughter's perfect,
infant cheek would make
Stephen King nervous.

New Faith Rising

There is, of course, Saint Hildegard of Bingen,
that renaissance woman before the renaissance
who painted, wrote, composed, and saw visions,
but I am bestowing Hildegaard Welcher of Vermillion,
that Child of the Afternoon, who finds the smallest breeze
something to revel in, and drinks her milk like manna:
Patron Saint of Morning Mercies.
Because when I look at her in the morning,
I see what it means to be beloved of God.

All she has to do is grin.

I'm not Catholic. I don't pray to saints.
But as a Protestant I have *leanings*
and these *leanings* lead me to admire
at the least the *idea* of saints, looking to them
as that cloud of witnesses, a reminder of
who we are and can become. And Hilde
is the epitome of mercy; a gift we failed to
receive, delayed by cancer, death, divorce
and miscarriage. We held open our hands
to God, then closed them again, empty

Until that day.

Hildegaard Welcher of South Dakota,
Patron Saint of All That We Never Thought Could Be,
she opens and closes her hands around our fingers

and we remember what it means to pray.

She learns how to make the sound *"Nnya!"*
And we believe again. We believe in things
left for dead. We believe in a God of surprises,
and the saints behind us nod, humble yet knowing,
And the saints before us wait, holding their breath.
Saint Hildegaard of the Midwestern Prairie,

Patron Saint of New Faith Rising,
Patron Saint of All Things New.

Eleven Percent

They say that only
eleven percent of infants
smile socially by two weeks
old, but I swear you have been
smiling, eyes shining like a secret,
all morning long
in the early light.

Vows

Marriage vows talk wistfully of
"growing old together" by youngsters
eager for their honeymoon in St. Lucia.
They mean every word, they just haven't
seen those words play out yet. It's not
their fault. Marriage is an act of faith, a
leap of hope; a vow that makes promises
beyond what we could ever know for sure
in that white dress, with those shaking hands.

We are not omniscient.

That couple, sandaled and spray-tanned,
ought to gather all the shells they can find
on that white, sandy beach and make all the
love and all the mistakes in love on those
white hotel sheets. The growing old will
come soon enough. But the aches and pains
are only half the story. There is an intimacy,
a bond that builds up like stubble in the sink;
that softens everything, like fresh laundry,
and provides evidence of life lived, like coffee
grounds scattered on the kitchen floor.

The growing old is, perhaps, even better than the sex
and sand and sunburns of youth, because it is proof
that those perfumed vows, folded up somewhere in a

box of trinkets, safety pins, and old jewelry, has been
tested and found true.

Will you love me after I disappoint you?

Yes.

Will I love you after you disappoint me?

Yes.

Yes. And so much more, while I get the baby
her milk from the fridge, still half-asleep,
asking you for the hundredth time if you
had any good dreams last night. You say,
as always, that you don't remember your dreams,
but I don't believe you. Because this was a dream
you had once, and it came true. You smile,
and I put the coffee on while you
take out the trash, like a love song.

Praying for Birds

I spent the morning praying for a bird; a fluff of a blue jay sitting at the base of our maple tree. I was worried for him at first because he didn't seem ready to fly while my cat, Ronald, is always ready to hunt. I wondered if I should give him a nudge, but I waited.

As I waited, I noticed his mother and father nearby, taking turns swooping down to check on him. Mother Bird, who I identified by her subdued colors, squawked at me when I inadvertently sat down with my own baby under the tree. It's our spot. We sit there multiple times a day on a quilted blanket, surrounded by soggy toys that I forgot to bring in the night before. Hildegaard is sixteen pounds of eager joy and she loves to look up at the leaves and wait for her best friend, the aforementioned predator – Ron – to come say hello. Our routine is simple, but it matters.

Today, we deferred to Mama Bird, and moved to the porch where I continued to watch the little family as Hilde grasped at a stuffed ostrich, chewing on its beak. I prayed:

Father, help him fly.
Make him fly.

I'm increasingly tired these days. Not from motherhood or age, but from angst over the way we treat one another. In *Grey's Anatomy* – the extent of my medical education – the surgeons are always talking about tissues that have become "friable." Fragile. Difficult to approach without extreme caution. Lately, it feels like we're just holding our breath - all of us - waiting to be misunderstood.

Gen Z is brilliant but quiet. They have ideas and passions, but they have seen what happens when someone tweets the wrong thing. Or forgets to use someone's preferred pronouns or doesn't remember to pull up their mask in a Trader Joe's. Mercy is missing. In this New Order, judgements are final.

The brightly feathered Father Bird swoops down to give his fledgling a few gentle pecks. An hour later, he returns with food which he not-so-gently shoves down his baby's throat. After all this - hours of Mother squawks and Fatherly encouragement - the baby bird remains at the base of the tree. And I keep praying.

I sit and watch birds care for one another. Check on each other. Root for one another's flourishing. And Hilde smiles at the cat, grabbing his fur with her baby fists. She doesn't know how to hold a grudge, act passive aggressively, or try to hurt someone because they hurt her. All she knows is that she loves cats and milk and Carole King. She fusses sometimes, but that's because she has an immediate need: hunger, thirst, or fatigue. It's not complicated. She doesn't know yet. She doesn't know how friable things become as we grow older and stop watching birds. So I pray:

God, help us. All of us.
Show us mercy. And help us.
Show mercy to others in return.

Vapors

I cradle you in my arms in the tick-tocking
dead of night when no one texts back and
even the birds are asleep. We trade stories
of spit-up and "when they first put you in
my arms..." as the moon tosses back and forth
in her sleep. We are not asleep.

We have been awake for hours, taking turns
crying. You spit out your pacifier and howl
because you can't grasp yet, not the difference
between night and day, the meaning of life,
or your bottle. You are powerless to bring
comfort toward yourself, so I bring it to you
by placing your head against my bare chest.

Your squirming relaxes into noisy breathing.

I, too, am powerless to grab the moon by its
rocky hide and bring it down close enough to
give us sleep. But I can hold you. I can rock you.
I can sing broken verses from childhood hymns:

Jesus...
Jesus...this I know...
Jesus loves...

I start to worry about what this
sleepless night will do to waking day

until I remember that you are my day.
And you, like life, are a vapor that appears
quickly then vanishes, not into air but into
long, bruised legs, climbing trees, and
tangled hair and "No more kisses, mom."
Your baby fat will vanish. The cookies 'n cream
smell of your head after a bath will change. And so
I hold you to my chest like a prayer: *I love you.*

I'm tired, but I love you...
Jesus...this I know.

The Plague

The year we got the plague
wasn't a year, but two weeks,
and we held on by holding
onto each other, taking turns
holding the baby to our chests
because eight weeks is too young
to feel like this. We ate too much
Top Ramen and watched too many
seasons of *Grey's Anatomy.* You made
the characters say things they didn't say,
and I laughed and coughed and the baby
sometimes smiled in her sleep. We discovered
that she is resilient and stubborn like you,
And smiles at all your jokes, like me,
And lethargy doesn't become her.
We felt awful, but we felt happy too, because
we were sitting in the living room together,
whole and complete. We didn't know that it could
feel like this.

A Prayer for Those Waiting for the Other Shoe to Drop

Owner of Undiscovered Mountains,
I fear the smallest shift
In the ground beneath my feet,
In times of joy, I find myself
looking around corners
for what might be lurking there;
the next inevitable trial, temptation, or loss
waiting for me in the shadows
to tumble my happiness
to the ground.

I don't want to live in fear.

But I also don't want to be blindsided.

Creator of High Tide,
I have felt that peace that
somehow surpasses all understanding.
It is real. But in times of peace,
I can't stop creating possible futures
where everything falls apart.
Because I have seen that movie before,
I have felt it, deep in my bones, and I know
that it is part of this life, under the sun.
And that's hard to live with.

Lover of my Soul,
take hold of my quaking heart.

Everest

Today I watched a mom
brace her daughter as she
wobbled through the coffee shop
on a new pair of skates.

They held onto each other tightly,
eyes focused on the hardwood floor -
their Everest - until they made it
out the door into the sunshine.

And I realized that, one day soon,
I will get to teach you how to skate.

And now, it is the best day
because of that hope.

Being Known

In the middle of the night, as my daughter falls
back to sleep in my arms, I try a little experiment.
I whisper, "I love you," with eyes fixed on the
sleepy corners of her mouth, and I wait.

Her expression remains unchanged, in that
slack-jawed surrender that defines the "milk coma."
I try again, this time adding her name:

"I love you, *Hilde*."

Sure enough, her lips break into a grin,
eyes still closed, body still a sack of beans,
but there it is. Proof.
That she knows her name,
That she listens in her sleep,
That she loves being known.

I try it again, during afternoon naps,
to increase the sample size.
I nestle the words into a warm cheek
or one of her dimpled fists:

"I love you, *Hilde*."

And every time,
I watch her serene face break
into a smile, soft but distinct.

I don't know if she knows what "I love you"
means yet, or when she will or if we ever
truly understand what love is, but she knows
that I tell her "I love you, Hildegaard,"
even when I am bleary eyed and bone tired
in the middle of the night, rocking her back to sleep.

She knows that her daddy makes up songs
with her name in them when she is
inconsolable, singing about the origins
of her Broadway career, *Hildegaard the Star*,
making her legs kick the Charleston
until her tears turn into giggles.

She knows that we say her name
with light in our voices that didn't
exist before.

She knows her name.
And maybe that's all she ever
needs to know about love.

That it belongs to her.

Know This

I miss writing
but I'll write again.
I miss sleeping
but I'll sleep again (maybe).
I miss having hands
free, coffee, hot food
and hopping in the car
without a care, but I love
holding you more (always).
And not a moment with you
is a waste of time (ever).
Not a moment with you
is a burden. You are
exactly where I want to be
each moment (every. single. one.)

Know this.

Planter Box

It's still winter in South Dakota.

I get through it by kissing your cheeks
and thinking about the garden we will plant
come spring. I picture your tiny, bare
toes, scrunching the soil, and your small,
baby hands, shaking seed packets
like tambourines.

I can see a future where
you grow a little taller each week,
using your yellow, plastic watering can
to drench bright shoots of green;
checking every stem
of every tomato plant
multiple times a day, hoping
to find a tomato worm because you've
always wanted to see one, and because -
secretly - you hope to keep one
for a pet.

The truth is, I never thought I'd meet you.
I always knew you'd be a girl,
and that you would be magic,
but I didn't actually believe in magic -
that I'd get to hold you in my arms
and teach you to hold all things

with open hands, letting seeds fall
gently through your fingers
into prairie soul, and prayers
fall bravely from your lips.

I know that winter is hard,
playing indoors, getting tired of puzzles,
hoping to trade hot chocolate for popsicles,
and books for sprinklers. I know that
so often our seeds of hope
are covered in snow.
But you're my daughter.
So I also know
that you will see the potential
in every winter garden.

You will find your colored pencils
in the cabinet by the kitchen table,
spread out in your jammies on
a blanket in the living room,
pretending it's a sunshine picnic,
and you will map out a plan
for each planter box in our yard,
coloring every zinnia pink, and
every parsley leaf, the brightest
shade of green,
until spring comes.

You

As I watch you resist your
afternoon nap today, chewing
on your doll in a sleepy act of
defiance - determined to prolong
play time, I think about
stubbornness and sweetness:
how they make a strange pair,
and, yet there it is: you.

The Finale of Grief

I miss the ocean with the ache
of a coming kingdom.

And I miss the purity of a Church
I can only anticipate.

In a day or a thousand years
we will see all the creatures
we never got to meet this
side of heaven.

As a friend of mine says,
"We will finally get to
hug a bear."

And we will watch flowers grow,
the ones our yard rabbits ate away
before we could gather them into a bouquet.

In the coming kingdom, we will gather
the rabbits and the marigolds
in one scoop of our arms, and
sit with them under the same tree
where the lion naps beside the lamb.

Can you imagine?

There our tired bones will
settle down into the soft grass,

our fractured hearts will be mended
with everlasting thread.

And finally - finally we will feel
the conclusive rest of justice,
the satisfaction of bellies made full,
of shame evaporated,
sorrow eradicated,
the finale of grief.

All the family of God;
all of us adopted ragamuffins,
the former addicts of phones,
whiskey, and Amazon, of
selfish ambition, selfish sex,
and empty religious gestures,

The ones never picked first
will be at the front of the line
for heavenly manna. And we
who denied Jesus three times,
thirty times, almost every time,
will be given the keys to the
kingdom of God.

Can you imagine?

Acknowledgements

Many of these pieces previously appeared in my *Sketches* column at *Fathom Magazine* (a beautiful space for curious Christians).

My close friends and family have faithfully read my work for years, even in its roughest stages, including poems sent via text message at 11 o'clock at night. They are the ones who keep me writing. They are the ones who keep me sane.

I lost three babies through miscarriage over the course of writing this book. I also gave birth to our daughter, Hildegaard Mae. Evan and I long to see these siblings together one day, playing hide and seek on that celestial shore. Until then, we live with the idea of what could have been and look into Hilde's wide eyes to soak up the beautiful reality of now.

About the Author

Rachel Joy Welcher is a California poet living in South Dakota. She has two previous collections: *Blue Tarp* (*Finishing Line Press*, 2016) and *Two Funerals, Then Easter* (*Dustlings Press*, 2018).

She currently works as an editor at *Fathom Magazine* and *Lexham Press* and received her Master of Letters in theology from *The University of St. Andrews* in Scotland.

Rachel lives in a small town with her husband, Evan, a pastor and fellow poet, and their longed-for daughter, Hildegaard.

Made in the USA
Columbia, SC
02 January 2023